Praise for "How to Communicate"

"Anybody who reads 'How to Communicate' will see th_____ _____ _____ng special. . . . 'How to Communicate' showcases [John Le_____ _____ ability to leave the reader finding something new even after the third and fourth read. Every section offers something fresh and dynamic. . . . [H]e invites his readers into a world of texture and touch, with hopes they will want to stay. And they will."

—Victoria England, "RHINO Poetry"

"The collection is less about a message's content than about 'how' that message moves between the bodies who make and receive it. . . . The poems in 'How to Communicate' are too sprawling for the book itself; their ever-growing hands press beyond the edges of pages and up through the spine. . . . Reaching across centuries, Clark models a crip solidarity premised on innovation."

—Clare Mullaney, "Public Books"

"The poems in John Lee Clark's revolutionary 'How to Communicate' work together as a manifesto that lays bare the ways in which a society that assumes seeing and hearing as the norm views touch as suspicious, enough so to try to outlaw touch. And yet, if manifesto, also invitation: what might it mean to write 'forward in a different direction and from a different spatial perspective,' Clark asks, and goes on to show us, in poems of formal virtuosity, of fierce tenderness, of triumphant community: 'We take another deep breath. A gathering. We are ready to teach the world.' 'How to Communicate' is the steadily revelatory gift I didn't know I'd been waiting for."

—Carl Phillips, author of "Then the War"

"'How to Communicate' brims with the talent and generosity of a living classic. And what a talent! Take, for instance, Slateku, a form John Lee Clark has created based on Braille: it is both inimitable and available to anyone. Or take his brilliant prose poems that are completely unlike any other prose poems I have read. I say he is generous, and you can see that readily in his translations from ASL and Protactile. I say he is talented, and you can see it in the various tonalities of this book, but perhaps most obviously in his erasures, where canonical texts are instantly reinvented by the new voice, felt anew, who lives in many cultures at once. There is simply no one else like John Lee Clark and I envy the readers who discover him for the first time."　　　　　　　　　　　　　　—Ilya Kaminsky, author of "Deaf Republic"

"John Lee Clark writes throuhout 'How to Communicate' of being exoticized, pathologized, infantilized. Yet, again and again, we find him demanding beauty: 'No, I'm not lost. / Go away so I can find out / whether it's indeed spring.' He has built a collection around such architectonic insistence upon awe, joy. That he is frequently laugh-out-loud funny belies his often truly brilliant formal intelligence. It's rigorous, searching work. And it's also vividly affirming—as a poet, as a reader, as a member of the human tribe. 'How to Communicate' is a masterpiece."

　　　　　　　　　　　　　　　—Kaveh Akbar, author of "Pilgrim Bell"

"Clark writes sensuous, radically intelligent poems. They 'touch' in every sense, offering fables in Braille and painful lessons in how to read the human heart: 'We touch / you. You do not flinch,' the poet tells a Cubist sculpture by Jacques Lipchitz. Nor do these poems flinch, showing us a scar 'from a cracked bowl that begged to be broken,' and scenes of cruelty that instruct in forgiveness. Hard-edged, concentrated, and sophisticated work, thoroughly in command of its art."

　　　　　　　　　　　　　　　—Rosanna Warren, author of "So Forth"

"This is a rare and gorgeous collection powered by human touch. John Lee Clark's poems approach, feel, and detail what we thought we recognized—a tree, an airplane, and even Goldilocks—on their way to challenging and enlarging our understanding of agency, community, and, most of all, language itself. 'How to Communicate' is a vital and precious bridge made of language—and once crossed, it will transform readers' sense of the world."

　　　　　　　　　　　　　　　—Aviya Kushner, author of "Wolf Lamb Bomb"

"Yes, 'How to Communicate' pulses with distinctive language and artistry, but John Lee Clark's poems stay with us because they churn with vulnerability and a longing for meaningful connection. These poems surprise us with sorrow, and they make us laugh even when they are tossing many of us out of a train window, clutching our old, empty values. This collection reminds us of the fullness of touch and the power we have to choose how we read and write our world."

—Gary Dop, author of "Father, Child, Water"

How to Communicate

Also by John Lee Clark

"Touch the Future: A Manifesto in Essays"

How to Communicate

Poems

John Lee Clark

W. W. NORTON & COMPANY
Celebrating a Century of Independent Publishing

Copyright © 2023 by John Lee Clark

All rights reserved
Printed in the United States of America
First published as a Norton paperback 2023

For information about permission to reproduce selections from this book, write to
Permissions,
W. W. Norton & Company, Inc.
500 Fifth Avenue, New York, NY 10110

For information about special discounts for bulk purchases, please contact
W. W. Norton Special Sales at specialsales@wwnorton.com or 800-233-4830

Manufacturing by LSC Harrisonburg
Book design by Beth Steidle
Production manager: Louise Mattarelliano

Library of Congress Cataloging-in-Publication Data

Names: Clark, John Lee, 1978– author.
Title: How to communicate : poems / John Lee Clark.
Description: First edition. | New York, NY : W. W. Norton & Company, Inc., 2022.
Identifiers: LCCN 2022027409 | ISBN 9781324035343 (cloth) | ISBN 9781324035350 (epub)
Subjects: LCGFT: Poetry.
Classification: LCC PS3603.L36464 H69 2022 | DDC 811/.6—dc23/eng/20220819
LC record available at https://lccn.loc.gov/2022027409

ISBN 978-1-324-07479-3 pbk.

W. W. Norton & Company, Inc.
500 Fifth Avenue, New York, N.Y. 10110
www.wwnorton.com

W. W. Norton & Company Ltd.
15 Carlisle Street, London W1D 3BS

1 2 3 4 5 6 7 8 9 0

Dear Smiling with Two Dots
Dear Soft Smile
Dear Two Solid Thumps
Dear Two Quick Brushes

Contents

Author's Note 11

I
Slateku

13

II
Pointing the Needle

Line of Descent 23

On My Return from a Business Trip 25

Excessive Force 26

Trees 27

An Honest Man 28

Knitting 29

Rebuilding 30

Clamor 31

Cubist Statue 32

Three Squared Cinquains 33

A Funeral 34

My Friend He 35

III

The Fruit Eat I

The Diagnosis 40

The Rebuttal 41

The Transition 42

The Interaction 43

The Gift 44

The Mission 45

The Manual 46

The Culmination 48

The Valediction 49

IV

Who You

To Ask 53

It Is Necessary 55

Mrs. Schultz 57

Etienne de Fay 59

The Politician 61

Old Deaf Joke 63

Goldilocks in Denial 65

The Bully 67

Nicholas Saunderson 70

At the Holiday Gas Station 72

V

Translations

Peter Cook and Kenny Lerner: Need 75

John Maucere: The Friend 76

Patrick Graybill: Memories 77

Noah Buchholz: The Moonlight 78

John Lee Clark: The Rebuttal 80

Oscar Chacon: The Lumberjack Story 82

Rhonda Voight-Campbell: Solace 84

VI

How to Communicate

A DeafBlind Poet 87

Pearl 88

I Would That I Were 89

Oralism 90

Pass 91

Order 92

I Promise You 93

Morrison Heady 94

Sorrow and Joy 95

Spread 96

Treasure 97

Approach 98

Self Portrait 99

How to Communicate 100

Acknowledgments 101

Author's Note

Readers may notice that certain typographical conventions are not observed in the following pages. I used to employ italics, parentheses, and accented letters with pleasure. The English Braille, American Edition, code—EBAE for short, or, as it is still colloquially called, "US Braille"—handles those textual features beautifully. For example, it uses the same symmetrical symbol for both opening and closing parentheses. Or take how one specific dot means that the next letter is accented, making it similar to reading "caf'e."

But in 2016, "caf'e" morphed into "caf!%#e." What happened? Well, a group of well-meaning educators pushed for the universal adoption of Unified English Braille, a code that supposedly represents print more faithfully, as if it was Braille's job or possible for it to do so. It eliminated some intuitive EBAE contractions and rules in favor of a robotic approach. This "print first, Braille second" system has not one but two symbols for an opening parenthesis, and then a different pair of symbols for a closing one. It has multiple symbols for each distinct accent. And it meant texts were suddenly thirty-five percent longer. What would have been a two-volume book became three volumes; a magazine issue bound in three softcover volumes was now in four or five parts.

It is my hope that there will be a return to an elegant Braille-first co-language. In the meantime, I have endeavored to shape my text in such a way as to minimize the impact of Ugly English Braille. Avoiding italics, parentheses, and accented letters all help it read more smoothly. Where publication names and book titles are concerned, I have followed the style used by the New York Times.

I

Slateku

The Braille slate has two parts connected by a hinge. The back is full of tiny depressions and the other part has marching rows of windows. You set a sheet of paper over the depressions and close the windows over it with a snap. Picking up a stylus, you press down to make dots stand up on the other side of the sheet. You must go right to left so that the text reads left to right on the other side. Although this process is often described as "writing backward," I prefer to think of it as writing forward in a different direction and from a different spatial perspective.

The classic slate has four rows of twenty-eight cells each. This never corresponds to twenty-eight characters in print, because the English Braille American Edition code has one hundred eighty-nine contractions. The one that saves the most space is "k" standing alone, which means "knowledge." "I will do it" is twelve characters in print, including spaces, but it is eight cells long in Braille.

Often you are aware of writing two things at the same time because the dots you are making stand up on the other side mean something else where you are pressing them down. It is not unlike painting the figure of the letter "b" inside a shop window for it to say the letter "d" to the outside. Unlike print, however, Braille is full of characters, contractions, and words that are the opposite of each other—"d" and "f," or, if they are standing alone, "do" and "from"; "m" and "sh" or "more" and "shall"; "to" or the exclamation point and the period or the prefix "dis" or the dollar sign; "ked" and the suffix "sion"; and so on. The exhortation "still, just have character" is more of a palindrome than any in print—it is the same not only forward and backward, but also dots up and dots down. To write "so you have it" is also to write the ghost of "which and just it."

The brown paper bag
Is almost the greatest invention in the world
The brown paper bag with handles
Is

*

My son says let's race
So we fly
A little ahead
I decide to lose without losing him

*

Alexander Graham Bell
Thank you thank you thank you
Where would we be without you
As our big bad villain

*

Attention Deficit Disorder
Plowing dust with my finger
Feeling what we are
Flicking it away

*

Part one young
Question mother father
Know right name
Work some day

*

Andy was a plain Blockhead
Sandy was a ponytailed Blockhead
Somehow they became less blocky
Then Candy got a cute baby cap

*

Hollywood
Smoothly wraps
Hollywood
Soothingly warps

*

How are you
My old old old
Bending over with age
Friend

*

A spat
Always starts out with a kiss
And ends with a high five
Aren't we lucky

*

Walking right on the road
On a snowy night
With my boys
I've never felt so warm

*

Can
You
Feel
qarowouwh

*

Nature
Does this rock count
How about the sun smiling
In my hair

*

Prehistory
The French army wanted to talk
In the dark
Without making a sound

*

The first pig oinked down
To the house of sticks
That will soon burst apart
With one mighty bad breath

*

I met Superman
He was so skinny
All skin
And bones of steel

*

enswirl
the wow artist
must find armor
sent through zings

*

What a wild time
We all had
In the shower room
Playing soap hockey

*

Ah my kidful wonders
Oh my partnerly love
How light is the brightness
Windowing in through the stream

*

What is the point of travel
For a DeafBlind person
Other than the food the people the shops
And all that

*

When we say good morning
In Japanese Sign Language
We pull down a string
To greet each other in a new light

*

The mutant four-fingered carrot
Is in the pot and growing
Sweeter as it relaxes
Its grip

*

Wood duck
I feel for you
You never had hands to stroke
Your own wings

*

The greenest pasture
Is always
The one
I am in

II

Pointing the Needle

Line of Descent

Susannah Harrison, "Songs in the
Night by a Young Woman under Heavy
Afflictions," didn't touch him, but Morrison
Heady traveled by stage from Louisville
to touch Laura Bridgman, who
demanded that Helen Keller wash her hands. Helen
later touched many of us but didn't let us
touch her back. Thankfully Laura also
touched Angeline Fuller, who
touched Clarence J. Selby, who
touched the whole world, first in Chicago
and then in Buffalo. Who shall we
choose for next in line? John Porter
Riley. We don't know who
he may have touched. We know far more
about his white classmate, but we hope
that he touched Geraldine Lawhorn, perhaps
at an Ohio Home for the Aged and Infirm
Deaf Easter Dinner. Jerrie
touched too many to number. Robert J.
Smithdas, who was an elitist bully
hiding behind poems so beautiful they opened
checkbooks. May he tremble
in peace. Richard Kinney, who
joked that the armed forces wanted him. "The Army
wanted me to join the Navy, the Navy
wanted me to join the Marines, and the Marines
wanted me to join the Army." But his hands
oozed nicotine. I instead claim Marjorie
McGuffin Wood, "Dots and Taps," who
insisted she was no saint. She fought

until she touched every one of us
in Canada, including Mae Brown. But Mae
turned out to be Our Lady
of Untimely Death. So Marjorie kept on
touching until 1988. My father Lee
was then still in denial, so it was I who
later touched him, not him me.
Leslie Paul Peterson, whose
poems still tap my shoulders in autumn. Dear too
Melanie Ipo Kuu Bond, whom
Uncle Tim Cook called Momma Nature
because she was so down to earth. But she
called herself the Black Turtle Lady
because the race is not to the swift. It is to the
slow and sure, certain of who we are.

On My Return from a Business Trip

Let go of my arm. I will not wait
until I'm the last person on the plane.
Go away. I never asked for assistance.
What? I don't want that wheelchair.
I'm fine. Let me walk.
Let me feel the spring
of my fiberglass cane off the walls.
What? I don't want the elevator.
Leave me alone. I don't know what color
my bag is and I don't care.
No, it won't take forever.
Go away. I'm fine kneeling here.
No. No. Yes. See?
I told you it wouldn't take forever.
Now will you please go away?
What? I'm just waiting, like you.
Let me feel the air get sucked away
just before the shuttle pushes it back.
No need, no need. I can step off
by myself. Let me go. Let me go home.
Go away. Let me walk
with my bag rolling behind me in the sun.
Let me veer off here
onto the grass. No, I'm not lost.
Go away so I can find out
whether it's indeed spring.

Excessive Force

Feeling my way down the street, if I ever
feel the cold
kiss of a gun or the cold
nibble of a blade, I don't want to
break the law. I don't want to
inhale the sweet night air and
explode. I don't want to
kick the mugger down, my hands
clawing for his throat, all my blind strength
pounding his head. Nor do I wish to
fall to my death. Nor do I wish to
run away only to
ricochet through a world where every shoe my cane
pokes could be his, where every
passing breath could be his, where every
floating pair of eyes could be his, where every night would
stalk me with his phantom, and where such nights would
consume all my days.

Trees

I love trees that stay
away from me. But when a leafy finger
pokes my eye, I squint.
I'm willing to dismiss it
as an irony. A limb
that knocks my head because I didn't duck?
That turns my heart into a chainsaw.

An Honest Man

My best friend, a sweet man,
drove all the way from Mankato
when my wife left me. At the door
he stood as tall as I
and we hugged. Then he said,
"Look good you. How manage?
Can't imagine. If my wife left
for sure gunmyheadshoot will."
I gave him a don't-be-silly shove.
Before he left, I could feel him looking
at me. He said that seeing me alone
made him cherish his wife. He did,
but his wife left him anyway
and—well, he did.

Knitting

The loops on one needle are the things
I should have done before she went
with our sons to live half a country away.
Putting the other needle through each loop
is all I can do right and right
now. To make each blanket smooth
instead of corrugated like a tin roof
that doesn't provide sufficient cover, I must
purl every other row, pointing the needle
toward my heart as if to stab it again and again.

Rebuilding

My grandfather spanked her. Half the time
she didn't know why. He didn't have the words
to tell her. After she got married and gave birth
to three children, he wanted to say something
to us. His hands creaked to life, building
stories about buildings. The sod hut
he was born in. The red barn on the farm.
The basement he put his family in while building
a house above their heads. The Ramsey Hospital
where he was foreman and where we would be born.
The Ramsey County Jail we always pointed out
on our way to visit Grandma and Grandpa.
The bird houses in their green garden.
It didn't matter what kind of building
it was, as long as it was done with his hands.

Clamor

All things living and dead cry out to me
when I touch them. The dog, gasping for air,
is drowning in ecstasy, its neck shouting
Dig in, dig in. Slam me, slam me,
demands one door while another asks to remain
open. My wife again asks me
how did I know just where and how
to caress her. I can be too eager to listen:
The scar here on my thumb is a gift
from a cracked bowl that begged to be broken.

Cubist Statue

after Jacques Lipchitz's "Matador," 1915

You are the best one
in the museum. You don't
try to be real. You
are wise not to attempt
hair. You have no face.
Your clothes make you. You
were inspired by a youth
famous for pretending to be
a statue. He would die
five years later. But you
are still here. We touch
you. You do not flinch.

Three Squared Cinquains

The Reporter Is in Awe
of a DeafBlind man
who cooks without burning himself!
Helen Keller is to blame.
Can't I pick my nose
without it being a miracle?

Am I a Nobody, Too?
I am sorry to disappoint,
but I am. Yet nobody
would let me be one,
not even when I catch
a bus stinking of Nobodies.

One Afternoon, I Found Myself
walking with my cane dragging
behind me. I well knew
the way. There was nothing
to see. Everything saw me
first and stayed in place.

A Funeral

for Cathy Erickson, 1964–2016

Cathy is dead. Debra, thank you
for reserving the community room in your
building. We know you will bake like you
never have before in your life because our
Cathy is dead. Tricia, will you
bring your tasty taco salad? Mind you
don't slip on ice. Peter, for once wash your
hands. Our hands are holy because our
Cathy is dead. Steve, thank you
for letting Sheila know. We would love your
to-die-for casserole, Kimberly, because our
Cathy died for it. JoJo, don't you
just buy a pie. Make something with your
own hands. Make anything. Our precious
Cathy is dead. We will honor what you
bring. Rhoda, none of us
will be at her family's funeral. This is our
funeral. Jose, as always, thank you
for the weather forecast. Jason, that means your
famous rain poncho. Laura, dear Mary Lou
will pick you up. Get ready to pour
stories into memory. She would have been so proud
of this gathering. Jessica, thank you
for asking. Sadly, I won't make it. But you
all will tell us about it on DBMinn, where our
funeral will continue. We'll be waiting for you
here, where we can get nearer heaven.

My Friend He

is so fierce
ly independent that he
shied away from the auto
matic sliding doors and he
walked around until he
found a window he
could pry open and climb
through to get inside and climb
the stairs to my apart
ment so he
could refuse dinn
er because I cook
ed it and so we
could have a nice vi
sit

III

The Fruit Eat I

In the following erasures, I address ableism and distantism by forcing problematic poems by famous and less known poets to tell a different story. Friends have asked why the poems I use to make these erasures are all a century old or older. After all, isn't ableism even more rampant in contemporary poetry? There is a practical reason. Very little contemporary poetry is available in Braille.

The Diagnosis

an erasure of Henry Wadsworth Longfellow's "Palingenesis"

I, sobbing in the rolling mist,
Started for peopled days. In dreams
A faded, lonely promontory shed petals.
Belief exists. Cunning with its perfume
Working from youth, defiance. A phantom
Vanished. The swift surrenders leap into
The old dead heart of lies.
I will give, remembering my turns
Into foliage. Of what light unseen!
What, what, what, what, what, what
Will hold still without its end?

The Rebuttal

an erasure of Lydia Huntley Sigourney's "On Seeing the
Deaf, Dumb, and Blind Girl, Sitting for Her Portrait"

Guide, passion, catch what
Hath no speech. Unknown
Joys, power, and meditation's
Unfolding sky. Feeling draws
Heart and wildering language
Still without speech to
Mind. Philosophy fails to
Sway this future child.

The Transition

an erasure of Edwin Arlington Robinson's
"The Old King's New Jester"

You, eyes furtive, see faces obscuring sight. Your wrong
Changes. Our dialetic regarding unstudied contrition. These reduced days
Travel: Vague but not with a determining must-know
Glamour. You may give a returning ingredient one last—

The Interaction

an erasure of "The Letter" by "Currer Bell"

Now fingers eagerly bent light aside. That touch slips, falls, falls, pursues

The deep sun. Caught unclothed, the light comes. Is that messy stair

Tall? Around leaves glow a clustering dance of still-earnest fingers. Her

Task: write. Ask her where hangs that dark, dark sky that may

Yet flower. If one turns distinct, the broad but faintly stalwart face

Locks. A furrow might tell a picture and a letter. The tearful

Tears see in hearts. Seas pass by England's colonial but smiling weeps.

The Gift

an erasure of Norah Pembroke's
"Erin's Address to the Hon. Thomas D'Arcy McGee"

O brain, poet thou, I have the voice. My hand. Shame I've still to art. Art in our hand, true carnage. How well my heads, chasing me, tarnish jewels! They're my one name. Where measure this life? Monster, the gifted fling false genius. Genius eateth our bowl. Knowest thou all raised art? The touch wilt bless.

The Mission

an erasure of Julia Ward Howe's "The Prisoner of Hope"

The patient struggle free
In slow volcanic fire.
So mayst life be
Truth, setting the domain
Of still comprehending liberty.

The Manual

an erasure of George Meredith's "Martin's Puzzle"

Book, how well I understand
Your gladness.

Suffer'd a fool.

Why heart?

Well, the human fist
Can be designed with a savouring.

Why taste the books
Of turns?

I never solve
Crush'd complaining.

Thanks leave
Wonderful body hymns.

Fingers only
Ask.

Answer this: Should it select eyes
Fixed on eye?

So, Book, what must injustice
Again mark?

Engines permit tools.

Respect may perhaps bow
But I instead question.

Made together, the sky.

Stop discord properly.

A universe from heaps,
Kneeling.

The Culmination

an erasure of Laura Redden Searing's "My Story"

Generous instinct, were you
My hand I must
Think. The later brain.
My hands craving every
Learned heart. Nature, art,
World. In my memories
I thought of trust
Then all fear. I
Fell on my pain.
Hope shall in loss
Throb. My, my, my
Stand for the release.
A nation's groan beneath
Dear night. All right.

The Valediction

an erasure of Dante Gabriel Rossetti's "Beauty's Pageant," "Genius in
Beauty," "Silent Noon," "Hoarded Joy," and "Barren Spring"

What culminating marvels, full of moods! Form within
Love's movement stemmed joy again. Words

 Like Homer's hand compassed Spring's gifts. Sovereign wall,
Are wires indomitable likewise? Shallower power

Hands blooms and skies round with parsley. Silence
In blue is our companioned silence.

Not sweet but in fulness the fruit eat
I. Floats the summer free like

Turning sails. Now it comes. Life. Dead today
Is this serpent's face. Gaze Shrivels.

IV

Who You

To Ask

She was a wonderful girlfriend

She didn't have to but she started to learn Braille

I say started because she didn't finish

She didn't finish because I was the worst boyfriend imaginable

She was studying the Braille book she had ordered from the Hadley School
for the Blind

Braille has a simple version called Grade One and an advanced version called
Grade Two and she naturally started with Grade One

She asked me about a passage

I read it and it said See Spot run

I said stupid book kiddies and tore it in half

She said hey my book

I said SEE I Is The WaS SPOT run Ing run eD duh duh and tore it into
more halves

She gave Braille up and almost gave me up

Almost

She went on to learn Gaelic French Japanese Danish Spanish and became a
pioneer in written ASL

Braille she never touched again

It took years and being kicked out and finally being separated for two years but I learned to be a good husband

During the two years I was alone I read and read and read

The ASL words Braille and Forgive are almost the same so it was like I was saying forgive me while brushing my fingers over the dots

Forgive me forgive me forgive me

I was wrong

She did master Braille

The hardest most advanced kind

It Is Necessary

It is necessary for every boy to think that his mother is beautiful

Heads turned wherever my mother went

She smiled and said it was because she didn't know how to walk quiet in her high heels or because she had forgotten to keep her keys from jingling

I smiled because I knew different

Then I met a beautiful girl on my short yellow bus

She got off at a different school

We made fun of the hearing bus driver who was a big woman with a mustache always eating out of a giant lunchbox

One day the girl asked if she could meet my mother because all the women she knew were hearing

I asked the bus driver to wait because I wanted to show the girl something

We ran to my front door and I flashed the lights

My mother came smiling under hair curlers and her face in green mud and she said nice meeting you to the girl

The next day the girl said your mother ugly same bus driver

She got off at her school

When the bus drew up to my school I didn't move

The bus driver asked me what was the matter and patted my back and
opened her lunchbox and gave me half of a huge cookie

Mrs. Schultz

The Deaf children never called me Mrs. Schultz

They called me The Oralist but that's not true

I do support Signing Exact English

None of them liked me except for one boy who I thought was too cheeky

He had Deaf parents too

I suppose that explains why I always found his hearing aids turned off

I told him you know the rules you need to hear if you are going to grow up

But he never listened to me

Sometimes he wouldn't even look up when I waved for the class's attention

I will never forget that day I asked the class to make penguins and to give
them to their parents

I passed out milk cartons for them to glue construction paper on

First the black outline then the white chest and eyes and then the orange
beak right there and two duckling feet here and here

At the end of class all the children carried off their penguins but the Clark
boy came up and gave his penguin to me

I asked him is this for me

He frowned and nodded as if to say of course

Dear me I saw right then and there what a sweet boy he really was

When his mother came to pick him up I told her how very nice her boy was
to give me this gift

Johnny saw me say that and exclaimed that he didn't know it was a present

I realized it wasn't just that he was shy about liking me but that I'd made a
mistake telling his mother that her boy wanted to give it to me

After all those years I still have his penguin on my desk and every time I
look at it I know why I am a teacher of the Deaf

Etienne de Fay

1669–1747

He got a little famous once

How it happened was the monks at Saint-Jean d'Amiens Abbey got tired of
their old building

And who else but their clever mute artist should draw up the plans and take
charge of its reconstruction

So the man who had learned at the abbey writing reading numbers geometry
mechanics drawing architecture history holy and profane especially of
France got busy

He went to the quarry with Brother Claude and Pere Postel and squinted in
the sun and pointed here and there

After twelve years of drawing and squinting in the sun and explaining
himself very well the abbey sparkled

Magnificent magnificent they all said the most beautiful house in the town

It was a memorable day when Pere Postel wrote in his diary March the
eighth in the year of Our Lord seventeen hundred eighteen the Bishop of
Amiens graced us with a visit

He wanted to see Monsieur de Fay our deaf mute boarder to witness himself
of all the good things he had heard about him and after seeing his talent
and capabilities he ought to say that we had a true miracle among us

After smiling and bowing and explaining himself very well Etienne de
   Fay hurried back to draw up the month's lists of things he would buy at
   market for the brothers

And always there were Deaf children under his charge all of whom learned
   all the subjects and explained themselves very well

One of the pupils was Azy d'Etavigny and he stayed with his master for
   eight years

Then his father heard of the oralist Pereire that he could make the mute
   speak

The oralist Pereire said yes yes your poor stricken son shall be a beneficiary
   of my secret method and he shall be famous in all the land

The boy went to live with the oralist and he did become famous

Only the Deaf pupils remembered their master and told their friends
   about him

His Christian name got buried inside the house he built and would not be
   rediscovered for another one hundred and fifty years

But his real name never left our hands

The Politician

The Honorable Larry Nesvig strode to the podium and Linda Gallea our
resident interpreter followed him and stood at a respectful distance

He opened his address to the Class of 1997 of the Minnesota State Academy
for the Deaf by joking that he knew a little sign language

He gave us a thumbs up

We snorted

He said that when he was in the Air Force he learned another one

He said when we really mean it we do the double decker thumbs up

He made a thumbs up with his other hand and inserted it into the butt end
of the first one

We gasped and laughed

He was delighted with himself and decided to plumb it for all it was worth

He kept the double decker thumbs up there as he spoke lifting it up now and
then to shake it

You all have done a constipation job and I am sure you will have a
constipation future and don't forget to vote for me because you know I'm
your constipation senator

We were choking by the time the Honorable Larry Nesvig lifted what he
    didn't know high above his head smiling like he couldn't believe his luck

We couldn't either

Old Deaf Joke

A Russian and a Cuban and an American were on a train

It quickly came to pass that the Russian took out a bottle of vodka and after
a few swigs he tossed it out the window

The other two men exclaimed why throw still have vodka good waste why

The Russian opened his fur coat and showed them rows and rows of bottles
and he said there Russia vodka plenty

The two men said oh and settled back in their seats

After a while the Cuban took out a cigar and after a few puffs he tossed it
out the window

The other two men exclaimed why throw still have left good cigar waste why

The Cuban opened his suit and showed them rows and rows of cigars and he
said there Cuba cigars plenty

The two men said oh and settled back in their seats

After a while a young man came whistling into the car from the next one

The American grabbed him by the collar and belt and tossed him out
the window

The other two men exclaimed why throw still young good man waste why

The American made an expansive sweep with his hands and said here
    America hearing people plenty

The two other men said oh and settled back in their seats

Goldilocks in Denial

Goldilocks was in deep denial and refused to use a white cane

That's how she got lost in the woods stumbling over tree roots and things

Then she hit a wall

A house

Door

She entered and wrinkled her nose and remembered the Annie movie from
   when she was little

It was the part where Daddy Warbucks said I smell a wet dog

It was dark inside so she did her ginger duck walk and zombie arms until she
   came against a table with some food on it

After emptying a bag of Doritos she wandered deeper into the house

Kitchen bathroom living room small chair too small medium sized chair
   too hard big recliner ahh that's much better

When the three bears got home they were happy to find that they
   had company

Papa Bear shook Goldilocks awake and asked who you

When she didn't answer Papa Bear put his paw under her hand

She snatched her hand back and said I can see

Papa Bear said okay and asked again who you

She said I'm from Long Island here vacation

Papa Bear asked when arrive here you

She said my name yellowcurls

Papa Bear asked need help you

She said will soon graduate May

Papa Bear gave up and turned to Mama Bear and said denial obvious
misunderstand misunderstand

Mama Bear said sad yes nothing can do leave alone

Baby Bear asked if he could play with yellowcurls

Mama Bear thought about it and said no better not yellowcurls denial
means hard talk can't play good

So the whole bear clan went about their business as if Goldilocks wasn't
sitting there

She jumped up and stamped her feet and said not nice you ignore avoid me

She whirled around to make a dramatic exit but ended up in the bedroom
where she stumbled and fell into a bed

She stayed on the bed for a long time pretending that she had planned to
sleep there all along

The Bully

We boys were marching up to Rodman Hall for supper when he stopped
and I bumped into him

He whirled around and pointed at me and touched his lips with his middle
finger and slicked it back over his head

I protested

He said yes you touch my butt

I said accident not see

He said not believe you

Before breakfast next morning he saw me watching Gilligan's Island

He switched the channel

Hey

He laughed

Next morning he did the same thing

I said oh that better thank you

He frowned and pressed the remote

That interesting awesome

Switch switch switch

Then Gilligan's Island was back on and I said no no not that

He laughed and left Gilligan's Island on

One time I was in the shower room and a rocket of water slammed into me

Fire extinguisher

I couldn't see anything except for a baseball cap

It was his cap

I laughed and said more more feel good come on

His last year I was still learning the art of the white cane

Sometimes I got delayed tapping around for landmarks

One night I was tapping between Noyes Hall and Frechette Hall and a boy offered his arm

I didn't know who until under a lamp I saw a baseball cap

Inside Frechette Hall I thanked him and he smiled

A few minutes later Gary Karow our houseparent came up to me and told me that the bully was so happy that he had helped me

A week before he graduated he grabbed my bag of books while my nose was buried in a book

As I searched for it he gave the bag back and said that he did it because I wasn't paying attention

His last words to me before leaving were you take care man

Some years later he drove down to Texas with a friend to help him pick up a
pickup truck

On his way back alone it was twilight and still in Texas when he turned off
his headlights

He steered into oncoming traffic

A car swerved in time

Another swerved

Then it was a truck which couldn't swerve and that baseball cap

Nicholas Saunderson

1682–1739

We are in the cemetery of St. John the Baptist Church

Can you feel what it says on this tombstone

That's right

That's how Nicholas Saunderson learned to read as a boy

There was no Braille back then you know

But he did go to Penistone Free School where he was allowed to listen in

Then he somehow ended up at Christ's College Cambridge

He wasn't a real student but he managed to stay around

One day William Whiston who was the Lucasian Professor of Mathematics
said you know my father was blind too and he preached just fine so why
don't you give this lectern a try

So Nicholas Saunderson began to deliver lectures

Mathematics astronomy natural history and yes optics

He made a calculating machine with strings and pins and called it
Palpable Arithmetic

In 1710 there was an uproar because William Whiston said Christ was subordinate to God

They kicked him out

Now they needed a new professor and they wanted Nicholas Saunderson

But he didn't have a degree

Sir Isaac Newton and Edmond Halley said no problem and they told Queen Anne to award him a Master of Arts degree

The next day Nicholas Saunderson was named the fourth Lucasian Professor of Mathematics

He bought a house got married had two kids joined the Royal Academy and astounded visitors by doing blind stuff just like I'm doing now

Here put your hands on this spire

It was erected as a memorial to him

Go on feel what it says

At the Holiday Gas Station

Near the Naked Juices I passed
A man my fingers walking
Across his back he turned and held up
A box said what
Might this be I said oh
You're tactile too what's your name
He said William Amos Miller I said
I thought you were born in 1872 he said so
You know who I am yes you're the man
Who journeyed to the center of Earth
In your mind he smiled on my arm said do
You know that the Earth also journeyed
To the center of my mind I said
I never thought of that he asked
Again about the box I shook it sniffed
Said Mike and Ike is it fruit
He inquired not exactly well
I think I shall have an apple wait
You haven't paid oh
My money nowadays is no money he pushed
Outside we walked across the ice
To the intersection he made to go across
Wait you can't go across we have to wait
For help oh help he said crouching
Until our hands touched the cold ground
He said I said we said we see
With our hands I jumped up and said you're the man

V

Translations

Peter Cook and Kenny Lerner

Need

translated from the American Sign Language

Need, frantic need, eagle-taloned need
is a pumping drill. The oil sloshes
to the brim. The lid slams and it's a tanker
spewing smoke. It burps and hisses
into a truck. It barrels through highways. It pours
down underground. It's a gas pump and a car
and a stop and a refill and a continuing.
It pulls over at the side of a tall tree.
It chops and strips and grinds and pounds
until dead fish float downstream
and our need is a single sheet of paper
sliding into a typewriter. It folds and licks
and places three stamps and sends on beating wings
to a door somewhere. A man reads it and fastens
his chin strap, carrying a rifle as bodies
fall and things go up in flames. It finds him
and the coffin lid closes. As soon as it stakes
a cross in salute, the crush comes
squeezing the soil for more. Oh yes,
we need so very much.

John Maucere

The Friend

translated from the American Sign Language

The Friend wriggled out and stood, a smiling tree, his shimmering head turning left and right. A person came along and looked up and said, "Who are you?" The Friend said, "Come on, get a buzz. It's awesome!" The person said, "I don't need that," and walked off. "Wait!" The Friend caught up and tickled him, his fingers hooking him and reeling him in. The Friend promised he would be popular. The person said, "Really?" He wasn't convinced. The Friend poured it on, slathering him until he reeled. The Friend slathered and slathered until his head bubbled. Reeling in circles, he fell down. "Hey!" The Friend tried to wake him up. "Oh no! He's dead!" He scooped up dirt, dropped the person in, and patted it down. He acted as if nothing had happened. Then came along another person. The Friend perked up and waved.

Patrick Graybill

Memories

translated from what Graybill calls ASL haiku

All those Sundays
on the long road
toward the red-bricked chimney
at the Kansas School for the Deaf.

* * *

The cheap paint they used: a yellow
that pained my eye, a blue
that made me grimace, and a sickly green
that made me gag.

* * *

Oh no, not speech class again!
My singing hands seized,
stripped, whipped, and shoved
into thick mittens.

* * *

Grumpy Miss Kilcoyne
waddling past
as we nudged each other, pointing:
"Bulldog on the leash!"

Noah Buchholz

The Moonlight

translated from the American Sign Language

That night the moon rose
in the window. Its light
touched the pane and spread
over the floor. The girls
climbed out of their beds
and gathered in the glow,
where their hands came alive.
Their chatter filled their chests
with such gladness it flowed
out past the sentry girl
at the door and down
the corridor until it struck
the matron's ears. She rocked
forward, enraged, and thundered up
the corridor. The sentry girl
gave the alarm. They flew
for their beds. The matron
burst in. Her arm swung
and connected. A girl dropped.
The hand of the moon
went to the girl, tapping
her on the shoulder, tapping
to no avail. It withdrew,
gliding back to the window
and out. When the sun
came up, its blaze seething

into the floor, the girls
gathered again at the window.
They watched as the gardener
dug a hole. His shovel
put standing in the ground,
he lifted a covered figure
and let drop. Its arms
were crossed as it tumbled
to the bottom. The gardener
grimaced and covered the hole.
That night the moon rose
in the window. Its light
touched the pane and spread
over the floor. The girls
climbed out of their beds
and gathered in the glow,
where their hands came alive.

John Lee Clark

The Rebuttal

This is a description of a Protactile poem I shared with two dear friends. I am sitting in the classic Protactile three-way formation with Heather Holmes sitting to my left and Jelica Nuccio sitting to my right. Our right knees are pressed against each other, and our left knees rest against the next person's flank.

Throughout the performance, Heather's right hand is on my left hand and Jelica's left hand is on my right hand. My hands do the exact same things, in symmetry, so that they receive the same message. Their other hands rest together on my knee. From time to time, they react to my poem by squeezing my leg.

I note to them the title of the poem, "The Rebuttal." Before beginning, I draw their hands to my chest as I take a deep breath and blow on their hands.

The poem begins. I touch their upper bodies and settle both my closed hands on their chests near where their hearts would be. My knuckles begin to rhythmically press against their chests. It is a pumping cadence. I shift my hands, where each one now has two fingers extended. Those two fingers slide and press across their chests toward their arms leading down to my knee.

After a few slide presses, my hands scoot back to their heart to do more closed-hand pumping. They fly back to where I left off the sliding presses. Back and forth, my hands pump their hearts and push the slide presses down their arms, down, down, down. Pressure builds up.

When the pumping has pushed the slide presses all the way down to their hands on my knee, my fingers hook between their fingers, fumbling.

The pumping force now pulls up along their arms. Back and forth, my hands pump their hearts and tug press against their arms, up, up, up.

When the pumping has pulled the tugging all the way back to their chests, the pulling continues past their hearts, up, up, up. The tug presses wrap around behind their necks. There, my fingers spread over the back of their heads and begin to vibrate.

The pumping is abandoned, and my vibrating hands roar back down their necks, across their chests, past their hearts, and down their arms to their hands on my knee. My vibrating hands clasp their hands, and all six hands are lifted up, vibrating, high above our heads. A pause, the vibrating ceases. I slowly bring all six hands back down to my knee. A pause. The poem is finished.

Oscar Chacon

The Lumberjack Story

translated from the Protactile

So the lumberjack has a hat like that, with a button right on top of your head. And they have suspenders over your shoulders going down to here at your belt. Nice! Give me your hand like this. Good. So they have this axe, solid wood going up your forearm, and the metal part tapers off like your fingers. Sharp! And they have this device clipped onto your belt here. I will explain later what it's for.

On this particular day the lumberjack sweeps their cane across your leg. Foliage brushes past your arms. Give me your forearm, fingers spread. So their cane goes up against your forearm. They feel it all around and slap the trunk approvingly. They unshoulder the axe and make three crisp cuts on your forearm. Good. Their cane goes up your upper arm, away from the tree.

Remember the device on your belt here? Well, they press it and it makes a noise. Your forearm falls down. That's perfect! They come back down your upper arm and feel the fallen tree all over. Whoo!

The lumberjack goes bushwhacking again across your leg. More leaves and branches pass by. Give me your forearm, fingers spread. So their cane snakes down your upper arm and encounters your forearm. They feel around the trunk. Impressive! Three crisp knocks with the axe. They go snaking back up your upper arm. They press the device and it makes a noise.

They return to your forearm. What is the tree doing there, still standing? Scratching head. Oh yes! They hurry back up your upper arm, turn around, and take the device off your belt here. Give me your hand. So they aim this at the tree and press it. Its screen shows a hand spelling the word TIMBER. Give me your forearm, fingers spread. It shakes, wobbles, and falls, bouncing off the ground twice. The lumberjack returns to inspect your fallen forearm. Whoo!

The lumberjack is back on your leg, forging ahead in the forest. Give me your forearm. Snaking their way down your upper arm, they bump into your forearm. Immediately, they know this one is special. They caress the trunk and their heart leaps like your heart is leaping here. They almost swoon. Unshouldering the axe, they give your forearm the three most loving taps. Tap. Tap. Tap.

They go back up your upper arm, turn around, and press the device on your belt here. It makes a noise. They run down but find the tree still standing. They scurry back up, turn around, and take the device off your belt. Give me your hand. So they aim it and press it. TIMBER.

At the base of your forearm, the lumberjack is surprised. Still standing! What's going on? Rubbing chin. Could it be? Could it really be? Only one way to find out.

The lumberjack starts climbing up your forearm. They reach your leafy hand. They straddle your thumb and put out their hand into the mass of leaves to spell TIMBER.

Your hand convulses in recognition. Your forearm shakes and wobbles. It begins to swoon. The lumberjack stays nested in your hand until the mighty trunk nears the ground. They leap out and land on your leg as your forearm crashes and bounces off the ground. Whoo!

Rhonda Voight-Campbell

Solace

translated from the Protactile

The wind. The wind
is throttling. Is throttling
your slender. Your slender
arm swaying. Arm swaying
back and. Back and
forth in. Forth in
agony holding. Agony holding
on until. On until
warmth comes. Warmth comes
to climb. To climb
and caress. And caress
your stature. Your stature
all the. All the
way up. Way up
to your. To your
budding fingertips. Budding fingertips

VI

How to Communicate

A DeafBlind Poet

A DeafBlind poet doesn't like to read sitting up. A DeafBlind poet likes to read Braille magazines on the john. A DeafBlind poet is in the habit of composing nineteenth-century letters and pressing Alt+S. A DeafBlind poet is a terrible student. A DeafBlind poet does a lot of groundbreaking research. A DeafBlind poet is always in demand. A DeafBlind poet has yet to be gainfully employed. A DeafBlind poet shares all his trade secrets with his children. A DeafBlind poet will not stop if police order him to. A DeafBlind poet used to like dogs but now prefers cats. A DeafBlind poet listens to his wife. A DeafBlind poet knits beautiful soft things for his dear friends. A DeafBlind poet doesn't believe in "contributing to society."

dead. I would be perfect for the temporary position. There would be no forms to fill out. My presence would be my signature. Things here in this world are so different. United Parcel Service's packages are color coded. McDonald's buttons are not buttons. The temp agency's tablets are tablets. I have wept in their parking lots until the tar got into my eyes. I have sat on committees for free. I have visited classes for free. I have been filmed and photographed for free. It costs so much to smile. I would that I were a candle wick in folklore. I would that I were a penny stretched over a railroad track. I would that I were a dragonfly curled up between your finger and thumb.

Order

We break our story into eight parts because there are eight of us to tell it tonight. It is our job to be one-eighths of ourselves. We break our audience into eight clusters. We shift from cluster to cluster. We don't do rows. We don't do circles. What we do is cellular structure. We are a living biology. Every part is different each time. Each cluster is different every time. The story is the same. We have been broken so many times we are unbreakable. We have been forced apart so many times we are always connected. That is our story. We are growing smaller and smaller and larger and larger at the same time. It doesn't matter in what order we get everything. It only matters that we get everything.

there's nothing in my face. There is nothing in yours. What we have are called heads. They are nothing unless we kiss. Lips are wonderful. They are full of mechanoreceptors. In the Old World we all used to kiss and kiss. It was then that we did have faces. We had noses and cheeks and foreheads and soft downy hair. In the New World we stopped kissing. Those who were already here stopped. Those who came stopped. Now there are only four people who have heads that are also faces. They are an artist and three children for whom I have a face other than my hands.

Morrison Heady

1829–1915

Morrison Heady was one tough nut to crack. It wasn't enough to have a splinter shoot from a chopping block into his eye. Nor was it enough to have a schoolmate playing catchers and leapfrogs slam his heel into his other eye. It took a magnificent horse bolting and a pile of rocks to send his head spinning. It would never stop spinning. He invented the alphabet glove. He invented a folding bed. He invented an adjustable chair. He invented a thermal pot so his coffee would keep hot and tasty. He invented a kind of gate so he could open and close it without dismounting. He invented a specialized Diplograph so we could emboss in Braille and Boston Line Type and New York Point all at once. He wrote a masterpiece in hexameter called "The Double Night." He journeyed to Boston to visit Laura Bridgman. He journeyed to Boston to visit Laura Bridgman again. He designed a blue cloak with a red trim so folks on the streets of Louisville would stay out of his way. He told fantastic tall tales so folks would flock to him. He wrote letters to all of us. Young Helen Keller called him "Uncle Morrie." He wrote novels. His publisher wrote a foreword to tell readers that they should be ashamed of themselves for not doing what this man was doing. Morrison Heady only said that his life would answer.

Sorrow and Joy

I am addicted to chocolate. I am addicted to chocolate. My pockets are nearly empty. My pockets are nearly empty. There's no sidewalk to Blake Road. There's no sidewalk to Blake Road. Wild animals don't like me. Wild animals don't like me. Insects do. Insects do. I am allergic to cubicles. I am allergic to cubicles. It took four months to read "Middlemarch." It took four months to read "Middlemarch." Adrean is a visual artist. Adrean is a visual artist. Our kids are growing so fast. Our kids are growing so fast. My Braille student showed up forty-five minutes early today. My Braille student showed up forty-five minutes early today. There are seventy-two unread messages in my inbox. There are seventy-two unread messages in my inbox. Time flies. Time flies. I didn't write a poem yesterday. I didn't write a poem yesterday.

Treasure

Our treasure is to be together. We used to be filthy rich. We had it as good as a ball of worms. We squirmed happily together in caves. We had it so good. We had our old curved nails tearing into pomelos. It was almost too much. One day a cluster wandered off and found something in the forest. It was too much. It splintered their souls into a million toothpicks. Some of them tried to come back. They stabbed us. They tried again and again until it was too many toothpicks to hold together against. We have never forgotten. Every time we snuggle against a wall we feel it. Every time we dig into a pomelo we feel it. Every time we wrap our legs around each other to talk we feel it. Our lost wealth. We want it back. We want it all back. The best way to get rid of a million toothpicks is by fire.

Self Portrait

on the morning of my forty-second birthday

The kneading of my broad swimmer's back by Adrean my beloved is the first gift. I nuzzle my pillow and inhale. I sniff my glorious hands. They take their turn at the giving. She says I am a furnace. In the shower I dig into my bestubbled cheeks. I scrape each fingernail against the right bottom corner of my upper left lateral incisor. My marvelous mouth pats the harvested skin into a soft dab. It rests tasteless on my tongue until I step out. My comb tickles my lips with a bouquet of pandemic hair. I sample the bitter end of a Q-tip and am satisfied. The fennel toothpaste searches me and tries me and finds me lacking in a few places. For Jael still sleeping I am a squeeze at their ankle. For Armand I am a known engulfment from behind. For Azel I am a quip and a laugh on his chest. For loafed and purring Angel I am a massive swoon. For hungry Nib I am two legs to rub against back and forth and to loop around with the most eloquently insistent tail in the animal kingdom.

How to Communicate

with Jelica Nuccio

They are so angry. They are so resistant. They are so thirsty. We need many breaks. We need another hug. We drape ourselves over each other. A deep sigh. You nod against my cheek. This is very important. A funny thought pops up in my head. You giggle and shake your head. This is very true. We take another deep breath. A gathering. We are ready to teach the world.

Acknowledgments

Fond squeezes for the editors of the following publications for keeping my poems:

American Poetry Review: "Morrison Heady," "Sorrow and Joy," "Treasure"

Blue Fifth Review: "To Ask"

Ecotone: "Etienne de Fay," "Old Deaf Joke"

Forge: "The Politician"

Jellyroll: "Knitting," "Rebuilding"

miller's pond: "Mrs. Schultz"

The Nation: "Eight Slateku"

The New York Times: "Pass"

The Paris Review: "The Interaction," "Line of Descent," "The Transition"

Pif: "An Honest Man"

Poem-a-Day: "Four Slateku"

Poetry: "Approach," "At the Holiday Gas Station," "The Culmination," "A DeafBlind Poet," "The Diagnosis," "A Funeral," "I Promise You," "The Manual," "Pearl," "The Rebuttal"

Poetry International: "Cubist Statue"

Rattle: "Five Slateku"

The Seneca Review: "Excessive Force," "On My Return from a Business Trip"

Shenandoah: "I Would That I Were," "Oralism"

The South Carolina Review: "Nicholas Saunderson"

Tin House Online: "My Friend He"

Two Review: "Clamor"

Wordgathering: "The Bully," "Goldilocks in Denial," "It Is Necessary," "Three Squared Cinquains," "The Valediction"

The Write Room: "Trees"

My translations also found their first homes in the following places:

Poetry: John Maucere's "The Friend," Noah Buchholz's "The Moonlight"

Split This Rock Poem of the Week: Peter Cook and Kenny Lerner's "Need"

West Branch Wired: Oscar Chacon's "The Lumberjack Story," Patrick Graybill's "Memories," Rhonda Voight-Campbell's "Solace"

Various poems appeared in the anthologies "Beauty Is a Verb: The New Poetry of Disability," "Deaf Lit Extravaganza," "The Nodin Poetry Anthology," "Saint Paul Almanac," and "Personal Best." This collection wouldn't be in your hands without fellowships from—and with—VSA Minnesota, Minnesota State Arts Board, Intermedia Arts Center, and The Loft Literary Center. Stomps also go to United States Artists, the Ford Foundation, and the Andrew W. Mellon Foundation for launching the Disability Futures Fellowships, whose inaugural class includes your friend.

Several overlapping communities gave much love: The WritersCS group, the DeafBlind Studies group, the GIPers, the contributors to The Tactile Mind Weekly and Clerc Scar, William James reading group, leaders of the Protactile movement, and my fellow pilgrims. If I began listing names, this book would be a thousand pages long. Nevertheless, for daily sustenance I am beholden to The Warmth of the Sun Within (Jelica Nuccio), Skipping With Joy (Terra Edwards), Two Assurances (Bryen Yunashko), Exacting (Cristina Hartmann), Booksnake (Oscar Chacon), Three Squeezes (CM Hall), Friendship Bracelet (Heather Holmes), Clamp and

Shake (Halene Anderson), Electrifying Happiness (Yashaira Romilus), The King (Jaz Herbers), Fierce Beard (Raymond Luczak), Gentle Beard (Gerard Williams), Community Nudger (Hayley Broadway), Dorsal Effect (Robert Sirvage), Dr. Holmes (Julie Evans), Dancer (Erin Manning), and my parents and my aunt and my brother and my sister.

Thank you to everyone who helped along the way, including: Alison Aubrecht, Jennifer Bartlett, Veronica Bickle, Sheila Black, Elisa Boettcher, Tashi Bradford, Noah Buchholz, Teresa Blankmeyer Burke, Roberto Cabrera, Deb and Brad Canaday, Karen Christie, Jim Cohn, Naomi Cohn, Shari Connolly, Peter Cook, Tim Cook, Dean Dykstra, Mary and Taras Dykstra, the Ekman family, Jim Ferris, Graham Foust, Frank Gallimore, Meredith Gill, Patrick Graybill, Timothy Green, Mary Hartnett, Christopher Jon Heuer, Sean Hill, Paul Hostovsky, Devin Johnston, Lilah Katcher, Mary Kirk, Christopher Krentz, Leslie and Myra Lambeth, Alicia Lane-Outlaw, Harry Lang, Lisa Larges, Maren Linett, Victoria Magliocchino, the Masgam family, Dona Mathews, Emily K. Michael, John Maucere, Michael Northen, Lois Pace, the Pecks, the Pedigo family, Carl Phillips, Christopher Phillips, Erin Ramsay, Lois Remmers, Curtis Robbins, Rosemary Sandford, Ralph James Savarese, Edna Edith Sayers, Vijay Seshadri, Don Share, Shari Stamps, Scott Stoffel, Pia Taavila-Borsheim, Leslie Ullman, Anna and Harold Van Sickle, Rhonda Voight-Campbell, Rosanna Warren, Cynthia Weitzel, Morgan Grayce Willow, Christian Wiman, Kathi Wolfe, and Pamela Wright.

Harry C. Anderson, Melanie Ipo Kuu Bond, Douglass Bullard, Mervin D. Garretson, Paul and Nelle Halverson, Paul Koster, Geraldine Lawhorn, Gerald and Kathy Meyers, Robert F. Panara, Leslie Peterson, my uncle Kenny, and my grandparents Alvin and Hazel, you all had a hand in the making of this book. Rest in peace, dear ones.

Michele Westfall, thank you for being the first writer I met and sticking by me ever since.

Thank you, Gary Dop. Yes, we all got dopped! Thank you to everyone in the Randolph College M.F.A. family, especially Kaveh Akbar, Chris Gaumer, Rigoberto Gonzalez, Marwa Helal, Ilya Kaminsky, Aviya Kushner, and Paige Lewis. Halene Anderson (again!), Cecilia Epps, Mitch Holaly, Vera Washington, and Donavan Williams, thank you for the co-navigating.

The Cyborg Jillian Weise, thank you for the shots in the arm.

Kristin Snoddon, thank you for insisting that I keep certain poems containing a device I now disapprove of. You're responsible!

Bouquets upon bouquets of sun-catching thanks for my stalwart agent, Tina Pohlman.

Jill Bialosky, Drew Weitman, and everyone at Norton, thank you for your care, company, and celebration.

Once more and always, to the dedicatees of my book—Adrean, Jael, Armand, and Azel, with our Angel and the Doctor rotating among our laps: My heart on your hearts.